The Art

yours in life

By Ted Dawson

Copyright 2015 by WE CANT BE BEAT LLC

Copyright 2015 by Ted Dawson.

Published by WE CANT BE BEAT LLC

wecantbebeat@yahoo.com

Table of Contents

The Art of Negotiating: how to get yours in life 1

Introduction 4

CHAPTER 1 – THE ART OF COMMUNICATION ... 12

CHAPTER 2 – THE NATURE OF NEGOTIATION .. 41

CHAPTER 3 – STRATEGIES IN NEGOTIATION 61

CHAPTER 4 – TECHNIQUES AND TACTICS IN NEGOTIATION 66

CHAPTER 5 – BODY LANGUAGE IN NEGOTIATIONS 94

Introduction

Negotiation has been a part of society since ancient times, many hundreds of years ago. People often traded products for money, clothes for certain services, or lands to receive peace. Nowadays, this concept has been reinvented and even changed its name. In this day and age, we call this habit "negotiating". Negotiation is a brand-new notion, as it has become an art. As is true of most forms of art, not just anyone can do it well. There are a few steps to follow in order to become an efficient negotiator. If you want something and know that you can get it through negotiation, you have to be really good at it in order to get so far.

Negotiation is more of a talent or an innate grace, but it is also a skill acquired through experience and intensive learning. Negotiation is a focused and interactive form of communication in which two or more parties currently in disagreement aim to find a solution that will eventually solve a common problem or achieve a common goal to the satisfaction of everyone involved. Negotiation enables the creation, maintenance, and development of interpersonal and social relationships in general and business relationships or diplomatic work in particular. They are often used for side effects such as gaining time, maintaining and improving relationships, and preventing the deterioration of the situation in conflict. If you master the art of negotiation, you have an extra chance to avoid hearing a "NO" from your partner. It means that you know how to orient yourself in order to influence and manipulate their behavior to make them say "YES".

Reasonable people quickly understand that they cannot simultaneously impose their own will and negotiate to find common solutions. Whether you find yourself at war or in the kitchen, in business or on the street, in a divorce or in a conflict with terrorists, you will have to consider this method. In fact, any form of human interaction puts into play a certain degree of strategy and tactics. Although there is no guaranteed path to success that will work in an infinite number of conflicts, strategic thinking and tactical action multiplies your chances of success most of the time. The strategy is a policy that may prove effective in a given situation but turn out to be completely inapplicable in many others. It is subordinate to the overall objectives. A strategic line aims at long-term effects and can be materialized by deliberate tactical actions or spontaneous, impulsive reactions.

The success of negotiations varies from case to case, depending on the objectives and approaches of every participant. To eliminate the risk of concluding negotiations with decisions that won't fully reflect the initial purpose, it is necessary to fix the beginning expectations and strategy that we use. For example, if our goal is to obtain a result completely within our own interest but in no way, shape, or form favorable to the other party, we must be prepared to resort to persuasion and assume the risk of not getting maximum benefits from the beginning. If we start with the idea that we can reach a compromise, the chances that the discussion will end with benefits for both sides are significantly higher. This does not mean that we should give up our goal or worry that our negotiating partner might get what he wants at our expense.

However, regardless of the intended purpose or the strategy chosen, the examples of approaches presented in this book are a good starting point for training for participation in effective negotiations. Why do we need this skill in our lives? Simply put, it is because everyone wants to make the most out of an offer or believe that they have. Everyone needs to feel that he has received a fair deal or one that benefits him. Negotiation helps us improve our communication skills and our ability to manipulate the actions of others and to take advantage of their weaknesses. It also helps us avoid conflicts and sets a common ground with other people. When you start a negotiation, keep in mind that there are many ways to do this and many styles that are suited to different personalities. Some are more efficient with a certain kind of person while others might fail outside of certain circumstances. This is why you should read this book in order to learn how to master this art.

First of all, you will learn how to communicate with people around you, how to listen, and what specific words you should use in certain situations. Communication is the foundation of negotiation. If one does not know how to talk publicly or wrongly transmits a message, the meeting is likely to fail from the very beginning. You will then find out that negotiation has many purposes and natures and learn how to differentiate them easily and effectively. Related to this are the models of negotiation that work on different types of people. Last but not least, you will be presented with some body language techniques that will help you to read your discussion partner and manipulate his answers or actions.

Settle down and take some time to study and explore this book because you will find a lot of useful information that will help you to become both a better listener and a better person overall. After all, our universal goal in life is to learn something new every day in order to expand our limits. Think of the chapter below as a certain key that will set you free from ignorance and limitation.

CHAPTER 1 – THE ART OF COMMUNICATION

Why do some people place barriers around their own communication? Communication is an art that can be learned only to the extent to which each of us gets to become aware of ourselves in relation to others, the environment, and ourselves. Another important aspect of communication is the subjectivism, generated by our own perception of the world and life in relation to our own being and our own expectations. Life shows us that despite our efforts to communicate "exactly" what we feel or think, others will sometimes fail to understand the message, emotions, or intentions. Then questions and frustrations arise, blockage occurs in the communication, and the result is conflict. Therefore, what do we do when we communicate? We say, explain, persuade, or act; we simply transmit verbal or non-verbal messages with disruptive or regulating effect. If we start from the straight definition of communication, it is a transfer of information from a sender to a receiver through specific channels that relies on the receiver correctly understanding the message. Who has not at least once happened to see what he wanted to see and hear what he wanted to hear, thus avoiding recognizing the reality itself? There is always the risk of extracting rapid conclusions. Many of us notice the antagonism between the two forms of communication, often unconsciously, in contact with others. In such situations, we often experience discomfort or hesitation in relation to the person. Even we will sometimes display contradictions between what we verbally send and non-verbally show: a state that we can often feel through our own discomfort associated with communication.

What should we do in this case? It is important to realize our own communication barriers in order to help us in our relationships with ourselves and with others.

What are these barriers? We previously discussed perception, the way in which we view the world and our relationship with it. We need to realize that our approach to communication is often influenced by our previous experiences, differences in age, nationality, culture, education, occupation, gender, temperament, and so on. How do we identify stereotypes or irrational beliefs? The only way is through constantly learning from our own experiences and avoiding falling victim to generalization, deflection, catastrophes, and absolutism towards others. Each person is unique, every situation is different from every other situation, and it is preferable to reserve the right to live here and now. We often forget that it can be difficult to effectively communicate with someone who has an education or life experience different from ours. In such situations, it is useful to ensure that we have the same understanding of the subject of the dialog. Everyone can assign meanings and hidden meanings to words or messages, and even our life experience can receive a special symbolism. Make sure you and your conversation partner refer to the same thing or that both meanings are the same. Ask questions to help the conversation. Ask for clarification, pointing out the need to understand your conversation partner or to make yourself properly understood.

Another frustrating barrier is the lack of interest from our partner. It takes time to get used to and accept the fact that we are often more interested in our own problems than those of others. If you can accept this, you should then try to develop a tolerance to this effect. Where there is an obvious lack of interest, we must act with skill in formulating the message so that it can meet the interests and needs of the one who receives it. Do not forget about emotions. Emotional distance can also form a barrier, and strong emotions are often responsible for the complete loss of effective communication. Remember, however, that it is natural to feel. Remember that to communicate is to feel and to convey emotions alike. By normalizing this situation, we in fact raise our awareness of what we feel in relation to the communicative approach in which we are engaged. Through practicing assertive communication and understanding the secrets of active listening, we can manage to identify or to externalize emotions in a manner beneficial to our relationships with ourselves and with others. Of course, each step or barrier can be a challenge, but you can pass through each obstacle supported by specialists in your classes of personal development, through life coaching, or through individual, couple, or parental counseling. Asking for support in such an endeavor means taking a step towards a healthier interpersonal life.

The ability to communicate is already an important skill in your career, and as you get into more leadership positions, it will gain even greater importance. Successful leaders are always excellent communicators, and it is impossible to exaggerate the importance of communication because everything you do revolves around it. You've surely already mastered the basic principles of communication, so the general principles discussed here will not be new to you. Chances are higher that in considering and applying these principles, you may identify some gaps that must be filled before you start to take the next step. Our attention here will focus on the ways in which you can improve your efficiency when directly communicating with others.

You've probably heard of the expression "art of communication", but you may simply not realize how difficult it is to master this art. Every day, we see people interacting around us, and we assume that the communication happens by itself. We tend to put equal value on quantity and quality when it comes to the way we communicate. A lot of talking does not necessarily mean a lot of communication, but it can often seem to be the opposite. It is a known fact that for all of us, the ability to communicate is an area that requires more improvements than we could imagine. Most of us think that we are already good enough at it, but sometimes, someone openly admits that he does not know how to communicate. If we all have such strong communication skills, consider the following:

- Why are there so many failures to communicate in our daily life?
- Why are there so many communication problems, especially in the professional context?
- Why are there so many misunderstandings and conflicts?
- Why do two people often hear the same message and eventually understand it in two different ways?

There must be an explanation for these and other similar failures. Therefore, we must analyze the problem in order to define the stages that help to improve your communication skills.

One of the difficulties that arise from the way we communicate is that it is perceived as a natural activity performed in one form or another since birth. Even in the absence of the ability to speak, babies still manage to effectively manifest their feelings. Do you wake up every morning and think, "Okay, now I'll get downstairs to interact with my family over breakfast"? You simply do it, and this requires little thought. This is a part of the problem, and our belief that communication is a natural process is actually one of the fundamental causes for our collective deficiencies in this area. In a sense, your approach to communication is similar to how you learned to ride a bike: at first, you thought that it was difficult and needed to concentrate on it, but it got easier once you got the hang of it. Now, you can simply jump on the bike and ride it. The same thing can be observed in what you do about communication. When you were a child, you spent a lot of time learning the words that helped you express yourself, but it became natural at some point and you stopped thinking about them. Now you do it only rarely and only when something goes wrong, but it is usually to blame the other side for the failure.

Seven Mistakes to Avoid in Conversation

<u>You don't listen</u>. Don't be like most people and anticipate your turn to talk; instead, just try to listen carefully what people say around you.

When you start to really pay attention, you can find a lot of topics to discuss in a conversation. Listen carefully, and *then* address open questions.

<u>You ask too many questions</u>. It is useful to ask questions, but if you overdo it, the conversation can begin to resemble an interrogation and frustrate your conversation partner. An alternative is to mix questions with statements. This will result in a pleasant conversation.

<u>You lack expressiveness</u>. In conversation, what you say is not nearly as important as how you say it. Tone and body language are vital parts of a conversation. Make sure that you:

- slow down. When you are excited, you are likely to step up and talk faster and faster.

Try to change this habit so that others can understand what you want to convey.

- talk loudly. Do not be afraid to talk as loudly as is needed so that those around you can hear you.
- speak clearly. Do not mumble. Speak perceptibly.
- convey emotions. Nobody will listen if you're dull, so make sure that your voice expresses your emotions.

<u>You enjoy being at the center of attention</u>. All those involved in a conversation should be the center of attention in equal measure. Do not interrupt when someone is speaking to attract everyone's attention back to you. Find a balance between listening and speaking.

<u>You must always be right</u>. Avoid creating arguments solely from your desire to always be right. Most of us tend to do that to an extent. It's okay to support your opinions, but try to accept those of your peers as well. Each of us believes we are right, and you will not impress anyone by trying to always have the last word.

<u>You talk about strange or negative topics</u>. If you're at a party where you don't know very many people, try to avoid discussing certain topics. It is not appropriate to talk about your poor health, about how your relationship is going bad, about your poorly paying job, about serial killers, or about any other subject that is discomforting because it might squeeze the positive energy out of a conversation.

<u>You don't contribute much</u>. It is possible sometimes to feel that you don't really contribute to a conversation, but try it anyway. Listen carefully to what others say, address questions, and make statements. Develop your sense of observation and learn something new from every addressed topic.

Now that you know what mistakes to avoid in order to improve your communication skills, it is important that you choose the three most important and work on them. Avoid making radical changes because you will become confused and will feel overwhelmed. Work on these aspects for several weeks, and then take note of any improvements. Soon, new habits will replace the old ones, and you will become a master in the art of communication. People will sympathize with you and will seek your company.

The curiosity trigger

The opening is essential to catching your potential customers with how many things you know about him. The approach has to transpose him into a world where he is or could easily be the main actor. Here are some examples:

For a personal development course:

- You have just been fired, your best friend has betrayed you, and your wife is to leave for France on a scholarship. Now is the perfect time to invest in your personal development!

For a set of educational materials:

- If you're one of those people who attract unhappiness and you start to doubt your abilities regarding communication, then this set of books is the step in the right direction you need to change your life.

For selling a trip:

- You have seen the world from north to south and from east to west. You have walked in the capitals of the most important countries on three continents. You have always searched that really special and unique place to which you absolutely need to walk. Finally, it is time to find that place. Discover.

A curiosity trigger has the disadvantage that it can discourage potential customers who do not identify themselves with the proposed scenario. On the other hand, the advantage is that the clients who identify themselves with these scenarios are easy to make loyal. It is one way through which you can address a very narrow market.

The final result

Direct and efficient! The final result is the simplest opening. In fact, it is an opening without an opening. The presentation of advantages is done directly, as in the examples below:

For a course in effective communication:

- "To be able to start a conversation in any place and at any time is a useful skill that you can acquire now".

For an educational package about writing CVs:

- "Write them, print them, and go straight to the interview!"

For a course on effective writing for promotional materials:

- "Apply the right model for your clients, send the presentation, and collect commissions!"

The opening through a final result has the advantage that it shortens the message. There are many occasions where a short message is more effective. In companies, decision-makers are busy people and prefer to receive as much information as possible in the smallest space. A possible disadvantage, however, is the loss of credibility because the client may think it's too good to be true.

Starters

If the openings are the packaging in which you will present benefits, starters are initial formulas for each benefit from the list. The reason why we need more starters is to avoid monotony. In a list with ten benefits, for instance, it's a little dull to begin each row with the formula: "How to...". To keep the reader's attention, you need variation. Therefore, here are some ideas for starters for a course on communication and influencing others through language. Initially, all 10 benefits were written with the introductory formula, "how to...". Then, we changed the approach and used different starters:

You will learn:

> *How to get along with your partner*
>
> *What the prerequisites for long-term relationships are*
>
> *What is meant by "double win" and how to apply it*
>
> *Thinking based on results for negotiation training*
>
> *The 10 Laws of Persuasion and Influencing and how to apply them in your work*
>
> *How to position yourself for maximum impact*
>
> *The seven words and phrases with maximum impact in sales*

How to make successful presentations

Proven methods that get credibility in little time

How to build a written presentation to have a great impact

Other possible interesting starters are:

- Reasons for…
- Key elements…
- Specific ideas about…
- A complete list of…
- 12 ways in which…
- … And the list could go on.

Another way of presenting the benefits of provided services is describing concrete actions using verbs at the beginning, as in the example below:

Prevent the loss of confidential information and intellectual property.

Monitor the reputation of your business processes.

Prevent the spread of inappropriate material in the workplace.

Increase employee productivity by restricting access to non-business emails.

Decrease excessive use of bandwidth, thus increasing network performance.

Words that have an impact

What we say can sometimes have the same impact as a dagger thrown into the heart of our opponent. It is said that words are weapons and language is sharp. On the other hand, in the process of influencing others, the highest share belongs to gestures and tone of voice. These are the basics of influence. Experts agree that the impact of words in communication is limited to less than 10 percent. Even so, there are a number of words that have a different effect. They are strong words, the force of which has deep neurological conditionings and the power to subtly influence. When used in phrases, they cause the listener to be significantly more receptive to proposals.

What does this mean? Some words are more powerful than others. The explanation lies in the social and cultural conveniences, in the way we were raised, and in our personal experiences. Some of these strong words are ignored and, unfortunately, they cause ignorant people to miss exceptional opportunities in life. Among the most powerful words in persuasive communication are found the likes of "because", "please", "thank you", and "now".

Name. The most effective influencing word is the name of the person you're talking to. There is a big difference between saying "How are you?" and "How are you, James?". The name is often used as much as possible in marketing and sales. In online marketing, newsletters contain the recipient's name. In election campaigns, powerful politicians like Bill Clinton or Tony Blair successfully use this technique when answering questions from the audience. You can use the name anywhere in the phrase to achieve the effect, but it is important to avoid repeating it until it gets annoying. Research also shows that the impact is higher when we use the first name than that obtained by using only the last name. The reason is simple: we all develop affection for our first names during childhood.

Another formula with powerful neurological conditionings related to childhood is the word "because". Parents often condition their children to listen to them by using this word.

A classic example is found in the following dialogue:

Child: "I want to go out to play."

Parent: "Later on!"

Child: "Why?"

Parent: "Now you have to do your homework!"

Child: "But I want to go out now!"

Parent: "No!"

Child: "Why?"

Parent: "Because I said so!"

This formula remains until adulthood and becomes a powerful "motivational hook" that leads us to do what we are told. It is important for all of us to realize this aspect because it will allow us to be better communicators.

Now. This word acts as a command: "now" is the time when that command or invitation accompanied by an advantage has to be honored! Consider three examples of using this simple word:

- *Now, let's get on with the discussion.*
- *If you are doing everything you propose now, you will feel like you made the right choice.*
- *You can decide to consider the most important advantages for you NOW.*

By contrast, let's consider the same example without using "now":

- *Let's get on with the discussion.*
- *If you are doing everything you propose, you will feel like you made the right choice.*
- *You can decide to consider the most important advantages for you.*

Don't you think there is a pretty obvious difference in impact when phrases contain "now"?

CHAPTER 2 – THE NATURE OF NEGOTIATION

The art of getting along with a conversation partner and avoiding conflicts or retaliation is called a negotiation. To do this, it's not enough for your partner to think and feel like you. You have to think and feel like him as well. You can negotiate the guest list for Saturday night with your wife. You can negotiate with friends on how to pay the bill at the restaurant. You can negotiate a salary increase with your boss. You can negotiate conditions for release with terrorists who have seized a passenger plane. You can negotiate the conditions to conclude a trade agreement with a customer. You can negotiate with the unions, with the political group in power, with the opposition, or with the delegation of another state. You can always negotiate with anyone. Negotiation is present in all stages of human existence.

In business, if you master the art of negotiation, you have an extra chance to win more benefits and keep a good relationship with your partner. When you negotiate well, you can orient, influence, and manipulate your partner to make him cooperate. The secret is to be able to train him in a game of "let's win together".

In the contemporary business world, negotiation and the negotiator acquire a considerable importance. For the manufacturer, importer, or wholesale distributor, a good negotiator can make in three hours the same as ten performers in a few weeks or months. A weak negotiator can lose much more than that. A small percentage change in price, the terms of warranty, delivery, and transport conditions, the deadline of a payment, or a margin of only a few dollars per thousand in fees and interest remain forever negotiable. In large transactions on the industrial market, where there are negotiated contracts worth billions of dollars, this negotiable margin can represent tens or hundreds of millions. From the position of each party, they can be either lost or won.

Definite aspects of negotiation

From the above statement, a few defining aspects of the negotiation process are evident: namely, the parties engaged in negotiation, their interdependence, differences between them, and their cooperation in addressing common and mutually beneficial agreements.

Parties engaged in negotiation can be individual negotiators or a negotiating team. Depending on the number of parties, the negotiation can be:

- Bilateral, when it is conducted between two parties: either individual negotiators or a negotiating team, or
- Multilateral, when more than two distinct parties are involved in the negotiations.

An example of a negotiating group is as follows: the heads of several departments within an organization determine how to allocate space in a new location so that the solution found complies with the requirements of each department. The negotiation involves transactions among many parties with divergent interests. On an international scale, multilateral negotiation is a form very widely used in conferences on establishing codes of environmental protection to be respected by all participating countries, for example.

The interdependence of the involved parties is the first condition of negotiations. People constantly interact with each other to participate in a joint project or to solve a common problem.

The mutual project requires the parties to join their efforts. For example, two neighboring countries that wish to establish a lasting relationship with each other, whether commercial, cultural, or otherwise, must take part in a joint project. Two companies that set up a mixed association have a common project. A couple planning their annual vacation engages in a project that concerns them both.

Common problems exist when there is a difference between the current and the desired state of the involved parties as well as some obstacles to overcome to get from the former to the latter. If these difficulties are related to both sides and can be overcome only through some level of contribution by each, then the parties face a common problem.

The idea of interdependence resulting from a common problem is typically expressed by the phrase "common interests". Negotiators have common interests in a given situation, which makes them hold talks in order to reach an agreement. In the absence of common interests, there would be a state of indifference among them and they would not consider negotiation.

The common interest in a commercial negotiation is the economic needs of the parties, which can be achieved by the transaction itself. Looking more closely at their positions, other interests can be identified: for example, the desire for everyone to be treated fairly, the desire to establish long-term good relations, and so on. With regards to the labor relations in an enterprise, the common interest stems from the desire of the parties engaged in negotiation to contribute to the overall objectives of the organization. Looking more closely at their interaction, numerous common points of interest can be identified.

Divergence is the second condition of the negotiation: in the absence of divergence, the interaction between the parties is marked by consensus. The involvement of multiple parties in a joint project does not necessarily mean that their interests completely coincide. On the contrary, there are significantly different interests between negotiators.

The seller and the buyer have enough points on which they disagree and should discuss, such as quantity, price, or quality. When a family plans how to spend their annual vacation and its members have different preferences, then they are left with no choice but to negotiate. If the husband wants to go to the mountains and the wife wants to go to the sea, then divergences arise within the joint project.

The cooperation of the parties, the third prerequisite of negotiation, concerns the possibility of exchanging values. In the context of interdependence, the parties agree to cooperate on the basis of principles and specific mechanisms. The fundamental principle of negotiation is "*do ut des*" (I give, if you give), or "*facio ut facies*" (I do, if you do). It expresses the idea that negotiation means an exchange of values. Negotiation is thus removed from situations of a unilateral transfer of value, such as instances of gift giving. In trade negotiations, the exchange is clear: a product or service is given for a sum of money, for another product, or for another service. In other cases, things also happen in a similar way. Sharing values is necessary for the parties, as with each being able to prevent the actions of the other, minor disputes may cause the mutual project to be aborted. For this reason, each negotiator must take into account both his own interests and those of the other party.

The seller must find out the real needs of the buyer and try to satisfy them; if this doesn't happen, the buyer can manifest his "veto" by giving up the business transaction. The buyer doesn't expect to obtain the absolute lowest price, which would be very convenient for him, because the partner cannot be forced to lose too much profit; focusing too much on lowering the price may cause the seller to manifest his "veto" by refusing the sale.

The definition mentioned another note of negotiation: namely, its voluntary nature. By this is meant that neither party may be obliged to enter into talks due to anything but self-interest and that any party may withdraw at any time for any reason. Thus, spouses argue and try to reach an agreement on the annual vacation because they want to spend it together. However, they can also end the discussion and either go on vacation separately or not go at all.

One way to better highlight the specifics of negotiation as a form of human interaction is by comparing it with other types of interactions. Negotiation is shown to be close to solving problems and pure confrontation. For this reason, human interaction is likely to develop along any one of these three lines: solving problems, pure confrontation, or negotiation. Those involved in communication will be those who opt for one of these possibilities. Negotiation as a human interaction is bordered on the one hand by the interaction of "problem solving", characterized by interdependence and lack of conflict and involving little to no divergence. On the other hand, there is the interaction of "pure confrontation", characterized by a lack of a common project and maximum divergences. The term "pure confrontation" is used to suggest that the parties engage in an open battle without any concern from any of the participants aside from defeating the opponent. According to the extreme to which negotiation is oriented, we can distinguish three fundamental forms: predominant distributive, predominant integrative, and rational.

Distributive negotiation is characterized by the participants' attempt to distribute gains and losses associated with the negotiated subject evenly, reaching a compromise. To use a well-known expression, "cake sharing" between stakeholders takes place. Parties endeavor to share the values and costs, their objective being to claim the biggest personal win possible. For example, two sisters who have one orange would like to receive the biggest portion possible, and they can get along by sharing it "brotherly" with each one taking a half. This solution is a compromise. The equivalent terms with the distributive orientation, used in different contexts and by various experts are:

- Negotiating in their own interest;

- "Zero sum game" in the mathematical theory of games: it suggests that a fixed value is distributed between the parties;
- "win / lose" negotiation suggests that by dividing the fixed value, what a party wins is a reduction of the value, therefore a loss, for the other side.
- Finally, the most commonly used metaphor for this guidance is "dividing the cake": the participants all try to get the biggest piece of "cake" possible.

Integrative negotiation is characterized by the participants' attempt to find ways to increase the overall gain that will then be divided through a compromise so that everyone will receive more. Equivalent terms with integrative orientation used in different contexts and various specialists are:

- Negotiating mutual interest;
- "Non-zero sum game" in the mathematical theory of games: it suggests that the amount distributed is not fixed, but is enhanced;
- "win / win" negotiation suggests that the parties can find solutions to increase the value so that everyone wins.
- Finally, the metaphor used for this guidance is "increasing the cake": the participants try, before splitting the cake, to make it bigger.

In order to increase the amount of cake, new values of division must be considered. Thus, the sisters can seriously discuss their interests. They may discover that while they both appear at first to want the same orange, one of them wants to use the orange peel for a cake while the other one wants to use the core to make juice. It is then clear that instead of splitting the orange in half, they might divide it so that each sister takes the part that she needs. In this way, each of them satisfies their interests and will be pleased with the results.

The rational negotiation is the one where the parties do not only intend to make or obtain concessions, but also intend to try to solve disputes from an objective position. This is why there should be clearly defined mutual interests without appealing to the slightest concealment or suspicion. The rational approach is all about defining problems, diagnosing the causes, and searching for solutions. The negotiator seeks to understand the stakes of his partner and to know his feelings, motivations, and concerns. Divergences that remain unresolved are regulated by objective criteria, societal, moral, or legal norms, or intervention by a neutral party.

The domains of negotiation

Many people associate negotiation only with the achievement of economic transactions or with solving disputes on an international scale. In fact, this mode of interaction is usual in organizations, in the social or political arena, and even in everyday life. Therefore, we can distinguish several areas of application, and the processes of negotiation will gain specific aspects of each of them.

- International negotiation

On the international stage, people often choose negotiation to put an end to misunderstandings or to establish and strengthen relations between countries. In other words, negotiation serves to solve present or past situations, such as war, or to prepare for the future, as with bilateral or multilateral cooperation agreements. The achievement of mutual projects like peace or cooperation is hampered by different views and interests that must be harmonized during the negotiation process.

- Management negotiation

Management negotiation covers those activities that establish, modify, and restructure social and labor rules within an organization, the ways in which resources are allocated, and how conflicts or problems are solved. In organizations, the role of negotiation has expanded as concepts and management tools developed, focusing more on participatory decision. This means that managers and contractors seek solutions to problems together.

- Social and political negotiation

Social negotiation occurs, alongside other mechanisms, to adjust the rules underlying relations between different social groups. The most obvious example is the negotiation of unions, which regulates relations between management and employees.

- Daily negotiation

In everyday life, people are often trained in negotiation processes through which they restructure cohabitation rules concerning them. Negotiation is a common practice and appears in various situations, even in our immediate vicinity. People often take part in a negotiation without even realizing it.

CHAPTER 3 – STRATEGIES IN NEGOTIATION

In negotiations, even more than in open conflict like war or sports tournaments, the strategy should be seen as a form of dynamic thinking. It becomes a way of approaching a delicate confrontation between two or more wills. Finally, if possible, the partners must think alike. Together, they need to get where they each wanted to go individually. If they can achieve victory without someone being defeated, then it is perfect. Negotiation strategy only works in order to guide and control, unnoticed, the interaction of wills in conflict, using both the cold logic of rational argument and the psychological energy of emotions and feelings.

Direct strategies

Direct strategies are used when the balance of power is clearly favorable to us, and the negotiation power easily imposes the strongest person's decision through a short and decisive battle. In classical military vision, the goal of these strategies is to accumulate forces and key strengths on the main field of operations and to annihilate in a decisive battle the bulk of the opposing forces. The maneuvers used are direct ones. The direct strategy is easy to practice when you are strong and face to face with a relatively weak opponent.

Indirect Strategies

When the balance of forces and circumstances are not favorable to us, we choose different solutions and psychological means to limit the freedom of action of the opponent. The indirect or side strategy is used when the opponent is stronger. To use it means to hit the opponent at his weakest points on the secondary fields of operation.

Instead of taking the initiative, we take advantage of our position of weakness through surprise strikes to his vulnerable points. The opponent must be removed from his strengthened position to defend his own weaker and less important parts. After their depletion from minor disagreements, key positions of great importance will be attacked. In negotiations, lateral maneuvering and means of manipulation are possible only with a big waste of psychological persuasion and suggestion that limit the opponent's ability to make decisions. Manipulation remains the only resource for those who are powerless and without a means of pressure.

Conflicting Strategies

The clarification of the conflicting or cooperative feature of negotiations is important for choosing tactics and techniques used at the negotiating table. Strategies based on force applicable under open conflict are simpler than the cooperative ones.

Conflicting or competitive strategies are those that seek to take advantage of the situation without making concessions in return. They are tough and tense, and they are always based on a disparity of negotiation power between the parties. Business relationships established through such strategies can be profitable, but not for long. They are strongly influenced by the changing market situation.

Cooperative Strategies

Cooperative strategies are those that seek a balance between benefits and concessions and that avoid open conflict, refusing to use aggressive means of pressure. When you find yourself using such a strategy, you should know that you have to face a partner and not an adversary. Cooperative strategies are based on positive influence such as promises, recommendations, concessions, and rewards.

CHAPTER 4 – TECHNIQUES AND TACTICS IN NEGOTIATION

When caught in the vortex of confrontations and quarrels, we control our impulsive reactions with difficulty. If we use the tactics, techniques, tricks, and negotiation schemes learned and practiced already, the chances of keeping control increase considerably. They help us to take initiative and recognize the opponent's tactics in order to administer the proper counter. If we can successfully discover the opponent's tactics and call them out, we can tear apart some of its power of negotiation. In addition, we have at hand a deliberate tactical line, a plan that deserves to be respected. Our negotiating power increases as we assimilate negotiation schemes validated both by theory and practice. There are hundreds of such tactics and techniques both in diplomacy and in business. Before proceeding to other theoretical and practical considerations, we will present a collection of tactics and negotiation techniques in the form of concentrated pills. The only thing you have to do is to swallow a pill when the situation requires.

Useful recommendations for negotiating:

- Before negotiating, you should prepare as thoroughly as possible. The time used for preparation is extremely rewarded.
- Establish your priorities and rank them. You will rarely be able to achieve all of your goals, so you must establish what

you can give up and what will be a deal-breaker.

- Start in force and give up slowly. Aim high and make small and slow concessions. Make sure every time that the opponent also makes concessions.
- During the negotiation, try to keep a balance between your interests and those of your conversation partner. It is not guaranteed that a tough and uncompromising position will get you maximum results, and if you are not careful, you can turn the other person into an enemy. A transaction does not need to have winners and losers. If the business is properly conducted, both sides can and will win. Most of the time, if the other

party doesn't win anything or doesn't have real interest in making the transaction, you too will lose no matter how good a negotiator you are.

- Focus on your core interests. Do not miss the interests for which you started the negotiation. These are the truly important ones, not the positions taken during negotiations. Pride is a good thing sometimes, but sometimes it is dangerous. Adjust your strategy to fit the situation.
- Compare the offers you receive in the course of negotiations with the alternatives you will have if you don't reach an agreement. Do not stick with unrealistic objectives you set for yourself.

On the other hand, an empty stomach is not a good political adviser.

- Consider the short-term and long-term advantages. It can sometimes be more convenient to settle for a lower short-term payoff when it comes with a guarantee or high chance of long-term gain.
- As a negotiator, your position should always vary between honesty, discretion, and misinformation. Negotiation presents very few situations in which you can afford to be completely open and honest without risking exploitation. On the other hand, if you don't give any information, you risk creating so much distrust that you will lose the partner in the negotiation.

- Pay attention to the feelings of those with whom you do business. If you offend or humiliate them, this might have more of an impact than anything else when they are in a position to make a decision. If they don't immediately find the chance, they will wait for the right time to pay you back. People never forget personal offenses.
- During negotiations, ask as many questions as possible. With questions, you can discover your opponent's real targets, you can get information, you can avoid conflicts, and you can convince.
- Do not get overwhelmed by the pressure of time. Your deadlines, if known, can be

used against you by the opponent. Display a lot of patience and make an ally of time.
- Listen carefully. Prove that you understand what your discussion partner says by repeating his words.
- Affirm your goals. To do this, choose the appropriate words and gestures that convey power and authority, but don't be too aggressive.
- Offer short proposals. When you receive a proposal, do not make counter-proposals in your turn and do not use the word "no".
- Multiply the variables of negotiation. The more variables, the greater the chance of obtaining a fair agreement for both parties.

- Confirm the agreed-upon terms. Never leave the negotiating table without reviewing each point of the agreement. Summarize each item in writing and determine how to resolve disputes.
- Build long-term relationships. Prove to the other party that he can rely on you and that you are rational and responsive. Seek ways to allow both of you to leave the negotiations satisfied. Be constructive.
- Analyze what you have done. Learn from past mistakes. Review the negotiations that just ended and look for areas that you can improve for the next confrontation.

Say NO as rarely as possible! Diplomats almost never say "no". After returning from his long journey in Asia, Marco Polo wrote that he attended the real schools where the ambassadors and spokespeople of Mongol princes and Tibetans were trained. They received in the evening the exact same number of rods on the soles as the number of "no" responses delivered by their lips. People hate to be negative, contested, or contradicted. "No" is a direct and categorical denial that cuts, tears, and strikes. "No" irritates and disturbs. It lacks delicacy. People tactfully avoid it. Expressed simply, clearly, and unequivocally, a response of "no" destroys options. It leaves no return, and it breaks the communication. Instead, wording such as "Yes, but…" can be used in the sense of negation, keeping other options available. It has three possible aspects: one that is "yes", one that means "maybe", and another that means "no".

Why say "no" when there is "yes, but..."? This is a welcome response in almost any situation. I think you will agree regarding a commander's reaction after he receives such a response, even if the answer is argued. More elegant than "no" is, for example, "Yes, I will resolve the situation but...", followed by a logical sequence of arguments that will demonstrate step by step that the subordinate is unable to execute the order. The secret of the "yes, but..." formula is that it allows formulating other people's opinion as a sequel to what the commander said and not as a direct contradiction to it.

False offers tactic - In short, the false offers tactic can be characterized as a bargaining trick that involves some theater acting. In general, price negotiation is a game in which one cannot win without the other one losing. If possible, opponents manipulate between them, even to the limits of loyalty and morality. One of the unfair tactics found rarely in textbooks and often in practice is one where the buyer makes an attractive offer to the seller to eliminate the competition and to motivate the development of the transaction. Once obtained, he finds a reason to modify the initial offer. Then they start the discussion through which he tries to convince the seller to accept a new, usually more moderate offer. The seller is often forced out of a choice by this point.

Another tactic often used by great negotiators is to **stress and nag**. This strategy weakens the physical and mental strength of the opponent. When negotiating with a difficult, unprincipled, and disagreeable opponent who is willing to uselessly engage in harsh and prolonged negotiations, it is recommended to use the trick of stressing and nagging. Many kinds of maneuvers can be used which, although they are not directly insulting or humiliating, serve to annoy the opponent, putting him in a position to hasten the end of the negotiations. Ways of harassing and stressing are vast. For example, take him for a prolonged walk inside the unit. You can accommodate him in in a room exposed to noise that would prevent him from sleeping. At the negotiating table, he can be placed with his eyes in the sun or another irritating light source. He can also be placed on an armchair comfortable only in appearance that, despite apparent luxury, squeaks so loudly that the caller is forced to sit still to avoid the noise. The examples may continue, but remember that these are methods to be applied only in extreme cases. When we are not interested in long-term relationships and intend to use such means of pressure, it is necessary that these maneuvers be made under the guise of innocence and helpfulness.

Another tactic, quite simple to use but unfortunately common in almost any environment, is **the bribery method**. A totally unfair method, it is based on weakening the opponent's psychological resistance by putting them in a position to accept small or large gifts. This tactic is favored when insufficiently motivated intermediaries conduct the negotiations for a separate party. There is a significant difference between protocol on the one hand and bribery on the other hand. There are some similarities, though. The role of protocol and gifting is to induce a favorable behavior towards the person that offers it. The little attentions placed on the negotiating table like pens, calendars, key chains, coffee, or drinks are, to a certain level, absolutely natural and designed to create a favorable environment for negotiators. Long-term business relationships can be compromised by bribes but favored by large gifts. The difference between a gift and bribery is psychological and strategic.

Time pressure tactics are based on the idea that there is always a negotiation program and an agenda of negotiators. These elements can be organized and manipulated so that a delicate problem remains when the time allocated for the negotiations runs out. For this purpose, you can use any tricks and maneuvers to delay and postpone. Towards the end of negotiations, things usually start to rush. One of the partners of the discussion will be pressed, of course, by some problems that do not allow for postponement. The discussion pace will then increase, causing one or both parties to begin making and missing errors.

The **small steps** technique or "salami slice" tactic is based on the idea that it is easier to eat the salami slice by slice than it is to the entire roll at once. If we ask too much, the opponent may feel overwhelmed and refuse at first. He finds it much easier to respond with a refusal. For him, it becomes more difficult to play the game without making concessions under too much pressure. Instead, by repeatedly getting partial benefits, armed with patience and tact, we can reach a safe and complete victory. Small successes may go unnoticed, but they will add up, resulting in considerable achievements. We don't have to find ourselves in possession of the entire salami in order to feed sweetly on it.

Alternating negotiators tactics adhere to the idea that when the partner switches the negotiator, you have to start everything over again. An early version of this tactic makes the negotiating team's boss look really gentle and reasonable but totally helpless in front of his team of specialists. In a deliberately prolonged way, the other team members are presented as tough, stubborn, and seemingly irresponsible.

During the negotiations, people from teams with various specialties are introduced in order to display a hard and uncompromising position. In this way, they create a psychological pressure with which the partner prefers to work only with the team boss and to accept the more reasonable proposals that disagree with those of the other team members. A second version of this tactic is the effective change of the negotiator. It can be a hard and unexpected strike because it is not nice to start all over again. The new negotiator is able to raise new arguments, revoke some of the agreements already made, or withdraw concessions from his predecessor. The new negotiator is usually the top man that takes you for granted when the predecessor hasn't already exhausted you. In these cases, it is better to adapt to the new situation and not get tired by repeating old arguments; rather, modify your attitude according to the new negotiator.

"Put the foot in" tactics are a minor psychological manipulation technique. In any negotiation, regardless of the subject or the identity of the opposing party, your goal is to convince your conversation partner that you, not he, are correct. You want to snatch a privilege, a concession, or an agreement. In order to achieve this, you influence his thoughts, feelings, and behavior in your favor. People manipulate each other in the most natural ways possible. The baby who whimpers or caresses his mother to receive a toy manipulates from the most innocent instinct. To a lesser extent, a gift or some flowers may be handling tools in the positive sense of the word. There are some major manipulation techniques like neurolinguistic programming and hypnosis, and a lot of simpler techniques used in such negotiations as everyday human relations. To cause someone to make a major concession, you first dig your foot in so that the door remains ajar. You ask for something insignificant but of same kind and hard to get. Only after that can you elicit the real request, which was taken into account from the beginning.

"Good guy vs. bad guy" is a good tactic for employers and union negotiations. The title phrase is the name of those tactics used with excellent results in wage negotiations. It is borrowed from detective films and experiences with long interrogations in which the suspect is passed from one investigator to another. It is also found in textbooks.

"The deliberate errors tactic." Its unofficial motto is "Forgive my involuntary mistake, partner!" People are human, and an unavoidable part of being human is making mistakes. In business, this general principle is sometimes used as an unfair bargaining tactic. Some deliberately "go wrong", sometimes in a long, premeditated fashion, with the express intent to confuse and deceive. Deliberate mistakes creep into written documents, in reports, in annex, in addenda, and so on. Most often, deliberate errors have as their purpose the replacement of certain words with others that bring additional advantages without exaggerating: for example, "net profit" by "gross profit"; "inclusive VAT" by "exclusive VAT"; "with adding" by "without adding", and so on. Many traders know the tactic of deliberate errors; this is why it's better to check twice before you sign once.

The **'hostage' technique**. In more veiled forms, the hostage tactics is found in various aspects of daily life and, of course, in business negotiations. It is ugly and immoral, but that does not prevent it from being effective. Hostage tactics are eerily similar to blackmail. The "hostage" does not have to be a person. It can be a document, information, a situation, a good amount of money, or anything important enough to force the opponent's hand. The rule is simple: the hostage is "captured" and held "captive" until the opponent pays a "reward" or makes a "concession" that cannot or would not be done under normal conditions. The reward or concession can be exorbitant, but the alternative is even worse.

The **"shutting the door on someone"** technique. According to this technique, in order to increase the chances of getting a favor from someone, we first ask another more important favor of the same kind, knowing that we will almost certainly be refused. Only after refusal, when the door was slammed in our face, do we come back with the request that we had in mind from the beginning. The chances of getting what we originally wanted grow considerably.

Statistical "intoxication". In most cases, the immediate and practical purpose of a negotiation tactic is to convince your opponent that you are right, possibly without directly contradicting him. To this end, it may be effective to exhaust him with all kinds of statistics: studies, extracts from the press, and selections of books, booklets, brochures, offers, catalogs, and the like that exclusively serve your own point of view. The rule is simple: never add anything to support the opposite view.

The surprise tactic. In negotiation, the surprise and alternating rhythm tactics are based on unpredictable changes of reasoning or negotiating parties' behavior. The sudden and unexpected hijacking of the direction in discussion, silences, surprising interruptions, launching of arguments, and unexpected advantages can have a bemusing effect and continuously intimidate the opponent, weakening his ability to react. The only thing that is important is to know when to change the pace; there may come a time when it is better to step aside and another time when it is better to attack. There will be a time to talk and a time to shut up; one in which to be firm and another to be malleable; one in which to take and another to give. You get patiently closer to the agreement and then move away to get close again, and so on. The opponent will oscillate between hope and renunciation. The surprise tactic can give good results against inexperienced or poorly trained negotiators who learn these negotiating schemas by heart. When they are suddenly removed from the script prepared in advance, they remain confused and rush to reach to some agreement in order to finish everything quickly.

"Time out" technique. Periodic interruption of the negotiation process by requesting a "time out" is a way to temper an irritable partner or to fragment and disrupt an argument. In addition, the request of a break when the opponent launches an attack or forces an unacceptable concession may be useful to prepare a satisfactory defense, to document, to consult, and to formulate a strategy to counterattack. In addition, the "time out" can pull your opponent out of his advantage, cutting off the offensive impulses.

"The short-circuit tactic." We will sometimes be brought face to face with a very difficult negotiator. He either possesses a psychological dominance that we do not like or is in a position of strength and hostility. In addition, he might be a highly skilled specialist in the issue of interest. The only solution that can save us in such cases is to avoid the difficult person. This is sometimes possible by raising the negotiation level to a higher hierarchical rank. This is called "short-circuiting", or "shunting the difficult link".

Paraphrase technique. In negotiations, to paraphrase means to summarize the conversation partner's statement in your own words. The fact that it involves his view should be mentioned explicitly. The paraphrase is introduced simply by sentences like "If I understand well…", "Let's see if I understood what you mean…", or "You mean…". With paraphrasing, we ask for further clarification.

The "questions" technique. Both questions and answers are a part of the negotiation process. As Aristotle once said, "the questioner leads". Any question has the character of a request, and the answer is a concession. The art of formulating questions and answers does not involve being right or wrong, but rather knowing what and how to tell or what and how to not say. In any case, a good negotiator knows most of the questions and answers that will be brought up by all parties before actually sitting down at the negotiating table. He behaves like a student who has mastered the subject and cannot be confused by the teacher. With well-formulated questions, you can always take the initiative. You can check and clarify the opponent's statements. Through questions to which you already know the answer, you can check whether certain suspicions regarding the opponent's attitude are grounded. Even if we get the agreement we desired, the partner may sometimes call the "trick" to ask one last concession. By doing so, he can get us mad, but all we can do in order to avoid an eventual mistake is asking a question such as "Are you suggesting reopening?" If he answers no, what remains is to respect the terms of the agreement already negotiated. If he does wish to reopen the negotiations, he will be asked another concession in return.

CHAPTER 5 – BODY LANGUAGE IN NEGOTIATIONS

Understanding body language begins with observing modes of behavior. Observation requires an objective registration of behavior. The observer shall have full availability in terms of mood because if he is overwhelmed by his own emotions, he cannot successfully perform these observations. He who wants to observe carefully has to be tolerant. We often minimalize the role of non-verbal cues and perceive only the tip of the iceberg in a conversation in which both partners have their own needs, desires, expectations, and aspirations.

Non-verbal language can support, contradict, or even replace verbal communication. A non-verbal message is closest to the issuer's reality, and it is the one that has the most attention from the partner. This is why we often find that although the party argues that he is telling the truth, we "feel" that he is lying. What is the "sixth sense" that receives the non-verbally expressed information from the issuer? It is believed that women have developed this "sixth sense" better than men. One possible explanation is that women are more capable of interpreting non-verbal languages due to the increased experience from raising children who communicate mostly through body language in their early childhood. Another possible explanation is that the development of this ability is to compensate for their lack of physical strength. Experts in the field have established the following report on information perception by the receiver in an oral communication:

- 7% words

- 38% - paralanguage (mainly intonation and inflection of voice)

- 55% - body language.

Non-verbal communication refers to the transmission of meaning through appearance, gestures, facial expressions, posture, movement, voice inflection, intonation, look, clothing, and so on. Body language helps the communication through facial expression, body movements, posture, general appearance, and tactile communication.

1. **Facial expression**. A lot of meaning comes from minor changes in the

orientation of the face. For example, a frowning forehead might signify concern, anger, or frustration; raised eyebrows with eyes open might signify surprise or wonder; tight lips might signify uncertainty, hesitation, or hiding information. A smile is a very complex gesture that can express a wide range of information, from pleasure, joy, and satisfaction to promise, cynicism, or embarrassment. Laughter, which is the limited response of a single behavior that reflects inner feelings, is an expression valid only to human beings. Laughter releases internal tension. The analysis of sounds in laughter indicated that laughter may contain one of the following vowels:

- A – open laughter from the heart; it is typical for honest people
- E – this is an ugly laughter, almost onomatopoeic; it is the expression of mocking, contempt, and scorn
- I – this is the laughter of people who want to seem younger; it is an ironic laughter
- O- this kind of laughter corresponds to some tense reactions; it is a defense from an individual that experienced something negative; depending on the

sound intensity, it can express anger, protest, and hatred

The ways in which we look at others and are looked at in return are related to our need for approval, acceptance, trust, and friendship. Looking at someone confirms that we recognize his or her presence, and intercepting one's gaze indicates a desire to communicate. A look can mean direct honesty or intimacy, but in some cases it can also carry common threats. In general, an insistent and continuous look bothers the person being regarded. Short flashes of contact often indicate friendliness. Looking to one side or avoiding looking directly at someone can denote lack of interest or coldness. Avoiding someone else's gaze means hidden feelings, discomfort, or guilt. Dilated pupils indicate strong emotions. Pupils widen, in general, at the sight of something pleasant or something to which we have an attitude of sincerity. Pupils narrow as an expression of displeasure. Frequent blinking indicates anxiety. The face is the most expressive part of the body. The specialists divided the human faces into 6 major types:

- Square type – considered to be energetic and active; has the will to achieve; authoritarian; conceited.

- Rectangular – needs work and domination, but it is more theoretical and shows less force in the realization of ideas.
- Long face – hypersensitive; pessimistic; meditative.
- Triangulation – cerebral; bold; original; adventurous; imaginative; unstable.
- Round - has a hot temper; sanguine; cheerful; optimistic; with transient sorrows.

2. **Body movement.** In literature, seven main groups of facial expressions were established, although each group has many variations. These expressions include happiness, surprise, fear, sadness, anger, curiosity, and disgust or contempt. These groups appear to represent facial expressions recognized in all human societies. Therefore, it is believed that they may be natural. We can say that every part of our face communicates: a frowning forehead signifies concern, anger, or frustration, a wrinkled nose shows annoyance, and a smile means the confirmation of availability for dialogue. Regarding eye contact with the speaker, it's about how the eye is drawn to the

subject. During about 80 percent of a conversation, our eyes are walking on the partner's face. Avoiding contact is a sign of shyness or anxiety. In an official meeting, maintaining a triangle between the eyes and the center of the forehead convey the message of seriousness and interest. In a friendly meeting, gaze is in the form of a triangle between the eyes and mouth. In all scenarios, the eye contact is important. If this contact fluctuates, the message is faulty. Proper eye contact means a continuous contact for at least 30 seconds.

A person looking up is currently visualizing something in his mind. A horizontal gaze means experiencing an acoustic mental process, and looking down reveals concern for his own internal state. For 90 percent of right-handed people, remembering something from the past is accompanied by eye movement to the left, and imagining future plans is accompanied by eyes that go to the right. Therefore, because this is an unconscious action, when the speaker talks about how much he worked the night before to finish his tasks while his gaze slides up and to the right, you have the chance to listen to a variant of what actually happened. Communication occurs through frequent tactile touch, such as shaking hands, hugging, and so on. Most of these gestures denote a familiarity between partners.

The arms and hands are "tools" in negotiations. In the rest position while the person is standing, they hang down freely. When sitting on a chair, arms and hands are relaxed in your lap or on the arms of the chair. The hand is the most commonly used appendage in body language. Hand contact is the culmination of preparations for the opening of trading. If you provide a soft and flabby hand during a handshake, the negotiation partner will consider you soft and easily manipulated.

Shake hands differently with different people. Hand contact, along with other signals, is a valuable indicator of personality. Rigid, authoritarian people will force the partner to return the hand face up. Conversely, those who reach the palm up have a defensive nature, always ready for unconditional surrender. Aggressive people, especially those who cover their uncertainty in this way, use hands like a vise. Avoiding involvement in the relationship is shown in rapid withdrawal from hand contact. This is what is recommended: comprise the entire palm and allow your palm to be comprised by the other's palm. The contact is firm without being rough, and hand peeling is performed at the same time as your partner. Normally, a handshake lasts three seconds. Holding hands in pockets may mean uncertainty.

People who keep their hands in their pockets show disinterest towards discussions or negotiations, and, in the case of official talks, it is perceived as a lack of courtesy. Touching the hand means pointing out when someone is lying or trying to lie. Of course, this should be interpreted according to the context.

Most unconscious movements of those who lie include comforting the chin, covering the mouth, touching the nose, rubbing the cheek, caressing the hair, or pulling the ear lobe. Taking the hand to the mouth expresses the tendency to possess us. This sort of motion is often in response to something reflected on the face that must be hidden or censored, preventing anyone else from gaining information from the expression. The head resting in the palm denotes boredom; on the contrary, a hand on the cheek shows extreme interest. When people feel frightened, they often feel the desire to have something in their mouth; the most common forms are smoking and chewing gum because they are quiet. Smokers often use cigarettes to calm and to control anxiety. Posture communicates primarily the social status that individuals have or want to have. A dominant person tends to keep his head tilted up; a submissive person will keep his head down. In general, bending the body forward means interest in the partner, but sometimes it means anxiety and concern. A relaxed position, leaning back in the chair, may indicate detachment, boredom, or excessive control. It may also mean defense to those who believe they are superior to their conversation partner.

Crossing the arms over the chest means withdrawal. Crossing the arms symbolizes a certain inability to defend, so it also includes a certain degree of subordination to the partner. It also expresses the need to defend oneself. For some people, this is part of a submissive gesture or expressing reverence to someone or something.

Soldiers in the army stay with strong arms and hands along the body. It is a posture that shows submission and wisdom without reflecting simple obedience. It means obedience to the role played in the given situation and towards a superior. The person who keeps his legs stretched when sitting on the chair feels safe. Standing with legs apart denotes indifference. The more the legs are removed from each other, the greater the indifference, although it could also reflect the desire to sit comfortably, a lack of discipline, or a lack of education. When a person sits cross-legged between two people, you will find that the knee of the covered foot is pointing in the direction of the person perceived as more sympathetic. A hand against the hip with the elbow pulled out is to increase strength and power that emanates. This posture is shown by the proud, arrogant people in order to produce the impression of dominance. When hands and arms are kept under the table, the person is not ready to cope; he is afraid to show his hands or believes that his hands will betray his insecurity, excitement, and nervousness. If your hands are on the table, it reflects the ability and desire to establish a contact.

Personal presence. You can communicate, for example, through body shape, clothing, perfumes, jewelry, and other accessories. Tall people are often put in senior staff positions that involve direct contact with customers due to the respect that is sometimes attracted by their height. Studies show that people with a pleasant appearance are considered more credible than those with less charm. An "artifact" refers to clothing, jewelry, perfumes, cosmetics, hairpieces, and so on. They are used as an extension of the person wearing them and to create an image of that person. The clothing can be used to create a role in negotiating situations.

Clothing and accessories can mark real or pretended social status. For example, women who attend a high managerial function will tend to dress in a sober two-piece suit and carry men's accessories, such as a briefcase. The best impression is given by wearing clean clothing. It doesn't matter if it is a legitimate clothing item of a particular style or an imitation of it. Clothing, as the result of personal choice, reflects the personality of the individual. It is a kind of extension of the self and in this context communicates information about it. For example, nonconformist clothing communicates that the carrier is original, socially rebellious, or a creator or artist. Brilliant colors are chosen by the active, communicative, extroverted people, but paler colors denote introversion.

CONCLUSION

From the ancient concept of trading to the modern art of negotiation, the skills involved in achieving our goals will always be an area that we seek to improve and that can have a powerful effect on our lives. Whether in business, international relations, or simply in our daily lives we will always need to communicate and negotiate with those around us. The more successful we are at negotiating, the more likely we are to achieve our goals and build good relationships with others. Effective negotiation is a skill that can be used in all areas of our lives and can have an incredibly positive effect on all of our interactions.

Successful communication is at the heart of all types of negotiation. Without first being able to communicate effectively we have no chance of entering into a meaningful negotiation. If the person we are trying to negotiate with cannot understand what we are trying to say then the process of negotiation will quickly come to a halt. For two or more parties to engage in successful negotiation it is of paramount importance that they are able to understand each other so that they can eventually reach a mutual agreement. Common barriers to communication include: a lack of self-awareness; a lack of mutual understanding; a lack of interest or relevance to one or more party; and a lack of connection on an emotional level.

In order to overcome these barriers and engage in successful communication we should seek to:

- Listen carefully to what others are saying
- Balance the amount of questions and statements in a conversation
- Be expressive and adjust our tone, volume and body language that we are using according to the situation
- Seek to allow everyone an equal opportunity to participate in the conversation

- Accept other people's opinions and 'agree to disagree'
- Change the topics of conversation so as not to dwell too long on negative or uncomfortable issues

Amongst the numerous aspects of what constitutes successful communication one particular element to consider is our choice of words. We all know certain words that can be emotive, hard-hitting or that trigger a particular response in the receiver. Most people subconsciously choose their words for specific purposes, like using simple words to speak to a child, business jargon with your boss and slang with your best buddies. To be able to consciously harness the power of words in negotiation situations can be a powerful tool to guide the conversation in the direction you require. Often we are looking to use persuasion to ease the process of acquiring our desired outcome from negotiation. Knowing how to phrase your words to influence the other person's response is an important aspect in the art of negotiation.

Research has shown that despite the use of words being a complex subject, simple adjustments such as the use of the words 'now' and 'because' as well as keeping a polite and respectful tone by using 'please' and 'thank you' can have a significant effect on how your message is received. Being conscious of the words that we choose, and viewing them as powerful allies in the art of negotiation, can assist us in creating a positive working relationship where successful negotiation can take place.

When looking to negotiate either bilaterally or multilaterally we should look carefully at these working relationships and how we relate to the other parties involved. Three main aspects can be considered: the common interest that has resulted in the negotiations taking place; the divergences and consensus of each party's interests; and the willingness of those involved to cooperate and compromise to reach a mutually beneficial agreement. It is important to take into consideration the fact that negotiation is entered into voluntarily and therefore can also be withdrawn from. To avoid a possible failure in negotiation relationships between the negotiating parties should be navigated mindfully and with a strong sense of reciprocity so that the communication continues and can result in a shared agreement.

There are different forms of negotiation that can be identified as well as different domains that negotiation can operate within. Skilled negotiators will take into account these differences when deciding the best ways to proceed with the negotiations at hand. Being able to recognize the form of negotiation that is taking place puts you at an advantage and prepares you for the type of techniques and strategies that the other parties involved may employ during the negotiation process. If we know that we are in a position of power over the other party we can employ direct strategies to achieve our goals and we can expect the negotiations to be fairly short and to the point. On the other hand, if we know that we are in a weaker starting position we can work to adjust the balance of power, for example by making concessions on less important aspects of a deal before attempting to negotiate to achieve our most important goals.

Sometimes we will enter into negotiations knowing that we are unwilling to make certain concessions or meet certain demands that the other party may be seeking. If we foresee that negotiations may be conflicting and competitive in nature we can be prepared for a situation where there is a lack of willingness to cooperate and apply a specific approach accordingly. It is important in these instances to be prepared and fully aware of our priorities and goals for the negotiation process. Without being clear on what we are willing to compromise or not we put ourselves in a position where the other party may take advantage of us and we may end up coming away from the negotiation table having given in to their demands and not receiving anything of value in return.

Other negotiations may be cooperative in nature and can be entered into with a different attitude. We may recognize that there are certain aspects that we can be flexible on, some concessions we are able to make and therefore approach the conversation in a way that is conducive to finding a balance between our own needs and those of the other parties involved. Such negotiations require a different strategy and different tactics to those used in a competitive negotiation situation. It is an awareness of the differing strategies and tactics that allows us to be skilled and effective in our negotiations.

As well as being aware of the tactics available for us to use it is also important to be aware of the tactics being used on you during negotiations. Some tactics are more devious than others and can even verge on being morally dubious. For example, the 'stress and nag' technique, where the opponent is tired or weakened through subtle interferences, can be easily criticized and many people would never even consider using this approach. Other examples include the 'hostage technique' where considerable pressure is used to force the opponent to concede to a deal they would never normally agree to. If you realize that these types of tactics are being used against you during a negotiation process you might have the chance to rethink whether or not you wish to continue with the negotiations at all, or it may at least give you some valuable insight into the nature of the people you are dealing with.

Other tactics such as giving a false offer, which you then amend or renegotiate at a later point, should be used with caution. So long as you are aware of the risks that such strategies can entail they can still be a successful route to coming to an agreement or persuading the other party to embark on a joint project with you. To really utilize negotiation tactics to your best advantage you should take into consideration whether you are looking to create a long-term relationship with the other party or whether you are just interested in pursuing your immediate needs. Some tactics, such as bribery, may work effectively for the short-term gain but do not provide the foundation for a longer-term partnership. More subtle tactics, such as the small steps technique, can be used effectively and without any harm to a potential long-term relationship. Some tactics, such as small gifts or saying 'no' as rarely as possible, can actually help to build a relationship and increase not only your initial success within that particular negotiation but also the chances of entering into future partnerships. By using certain tactics skillfully and appropriately you can gain your negotiation partner's trust and respect, meaning that they are more likely to select you for future dealings or even recommend you to other people.

It should be clear to us by now that the relationships we form with the people we negotiate with are of central importance to the effectiveness of our negotiations in the various arenas of life. The way in which we communicate can have as much as an influence as the message we are trying to convey. Therefore in order to be skilled in negotiation we also need to be skilled in the arts of communication, both verbal and non-verbal. Whilst choosing our words carefully can be a powerful communicative tool, it is reported that only 7% of any communication is actually transferred through words. That means that the remaining 93% of meaning is gained, mostly subconsciously, through signals given in body language and other aspects of how we speak. Here again we return to the concept that by having an awareness of these factors we can gain the upper hand and significantly improve our chances of successful communication and negotiation. By mastering our own non-verbal communication we are able to convey clear messages that are appropriate to our overall goals. Similarly, by being able to consciously read the non-verbal communication of others we can respond to those messages more effectively and in a way that will benefit us.

      A calm, objective approach to analyzing non-verbal communication can help us to gain valuable insight into the mind-set of another person. The role that facial expressions and eye contact play in expressing our true feelings is significant and it is often these signals that can give us away when we are being less than honest with someone. The way in which we look at someone can also 'speak volumes'. Think about how many times you have heard someone trying to describe an interaction that made them feel uneasy or as if something wasn't adding up and they describe it as 'something in the look in their eyes'. Being aware of these signals that we all give, consciously or sub-consciously, can again give us the edge in our interactions with others. We can even learn to notice the movements of someone's pupils in order to discern whether or not they are telling the truth. Conversely, if we are aware of these signals we can also learn to manipulate our own movements so as to more effectively disguise a lie or a half-truth.

When considering the role of body language in communication, we can use knowledge of common signals and non-verbal messages to better understand the people we are interacting with. We can even use this knowledge to ensure that even if we are feeling a certain way we can still choose to present ourselves in another by consciously altering our body language. One example may be feeling nervous or tense in a job interview and having the natural inclination to sit with our shoulders slightly forward and our hands clasped. Instead we can consciously relax our shoulders and place our hands in an open position, emulating the confident and calm attitude that we wish we were feeling. Being able to control these natural inclinations and act otherwise actually serves two purposes, it conveys the message you desire to the other person and it can also help to genuinely create the feeling. By 'acting as if' we are often able to generate the desired feeling, such as confidence in a difficult situation, and altering our body language plays a key part in this.

At the centre of successful negotiation lies an awareness of our own communicative actions and a willingness to understand those of others. Once we have this understanding we can then choose the way to best use this knowledge skillfully according to the specific situation and what we are trying to achieve. The insights provided in this book should help even the most inexperienced negotiator to quickly become a mindful and effective communicator with the potential to grow and learn through each interaction and negotiation that they encounter in life.

Made in the USA
Columbia, SC
22 January 2021